Learn To Code
Introduction to Computer Science
Workbook #1

Teacher Guide

A product of ThoughtSTEM

> **State Standards Correlations**
>
> See vox-l.com/standards to see how this book meets your state's standards for math and computer science.

ThoughtSTEM LLC grants teachers permission to photocopy the reproducible pages from this book for classroom use.
No other part of this publication may be reproduced in whole or in part, or stored in a retrieval system, or transmitted in any form or by any means, electronic mechanical, photocopying, recording, or otherwise without written permission of the publisher. For information regarding permission, write to contact@thoughtstem.com.

Cover design by Stephen R. Foster & Jason Rosenstock
Interior design by Carlos Herrera & Salvador Najar

About the Book

"Computer science is no more about computers than astronomy is about telescopes."
-Edsger Dijkstra

Professions involving computer programming consistently top the charts as some of the highest paying, highest satisfaction jobs out there! But currently, we just don't have enough programmers to keep up with industry demand. By making a version of Vox-L freely available to educators we hope to be part of the solution!

Each Workbook page contains a QR code like this one:

Scanning a QR code with a mobile phone or computer will unlock fun digital content and videos. These serve to reinforce the activities printed in this book.

Computer science takes practice. Learning to code is more about what happens in your brain than what happens on a computer. Think. Reflect. Analyze. Ponder.

Table of Contents

GETTING STARTED 6

USING VOX-L 8

VOX-L UI 11

USING THE FORUM 18

ACTIVITIES ON "/LEARN" 21

CARDS 25

CONCEPTS EXPLAINED 26

WORKBOOK ANSWERS 38

LESSON PLANS 47

Teacher Guide

Getting Started

This book is a complete guide to running a coding class using the Vox-L software. As an instructor, you do not need to be a programming expert, this guide will help you understand the fundamental concepts of Computer Science and help you develop the right plan to starting a coding class.

Throughout his book you will find explanations of coding concepts, a detailed navigation of the Vox-L Classroom interface and various sample lesson plans you can use in your classroom. Use this book as a reference for helping your students start a lifelong computational thinking adventure.

What is Vox-L?
Vox-L, originally developed to serve as a Minecraft modding simulator, is a web platform that allows the user to create, share and mod voxel--based worlds; a voxel represents a cube on a regular grid of 3 dimensional space. Similar to Minecraft, Vox-L appears as a cube based game. Vox-L has grown to be it's own platform for simplified use at schools.

We first built Vox-L as a testing environment for LearnToMod (another one of our products used for Minecraft modding), but we've since developed Vox-L as a separate platform for deployment on Chromebooks, Virtual Reality, and PC. It was specifically designed so that teachers and students could harness the power of Vox-L on a simple classroom chromebook! Vox-L Classroom is free to use and no account creation is required.

Coding in Vox-L
As mentioned in the previous section, Vox-L is intended to be a tool for STEM education, helping and inspiring kids to dive into the world of Computer Science.

Vox-L uses a drag and drop coding interface called Blockly. In order to write code, find the desired coding block from the left hand menu, click and drag it over to the coding canvas.

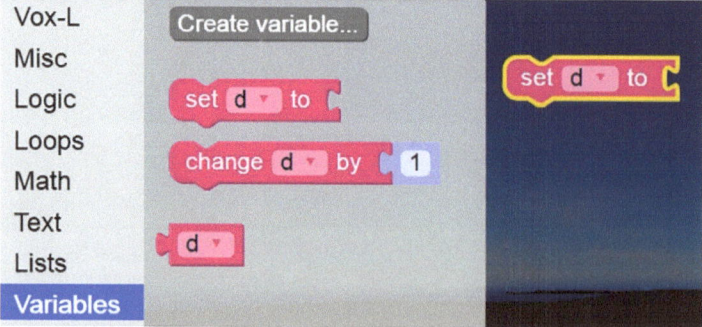

At ThoughtSTEM, we have found that using drag and drop languages helps students develop a visual understanding of how code is structured. This blockly language is directly translated to JavaScript which will provide a foundation for future programming languages they want to learn.

Who should use Vox-L Classroom?
The use of Vox-L classroom is recommended for students of ages 8 - 18 who want to learn how to make Minecraft mods but do not have access to Minecraft PC version.

The software is also recommended for teacher who would like to lead a coding class without the complication of software installation. One of the main design goals for Vox-L Classroom was its compatibility and performance within school networks. It is easy to use in schools because it is accessed through a website that does not require an account.

How is Vox-L Minecraft modding?
The same blockly code used in Vox-L can be used in LearnToMod, a subsription based Minecraft Modding software.

If you would like more information on LearnToMod go to learntomod.com

Using Vox-L

This section of the teacher's guide is intended to help you with Vox-L and is a quick guide to solving small problems you may run into.

Vox-L Classroom is supported on all major desktop browsers. Vox-L is not designed for mobile support. We recommend you use one of the following, confirmed compatible browsers:
- Mozilla Firefox 42
- Google Chrome 46
- Apple Safari 9.0
- MS Internet Explorer 11
- MS Edge 13

Controls

Movement			
Forward	W	Jump	Space Bar
Backward	S	Fly	Double Space
Left	A	Fly Down	Left Shift
Right	D	Fly Up	Hold Space

Actions			
Break Block	Mouse 1	Toggle Torch	T
Place Block	Mouse 2	Toggle Flashlight	F
Toggle Inventory	E	Hotbar Select	1 - 9
Toggle Code	Left Tab	Select Item	Mouse 1
Run Mod	M		

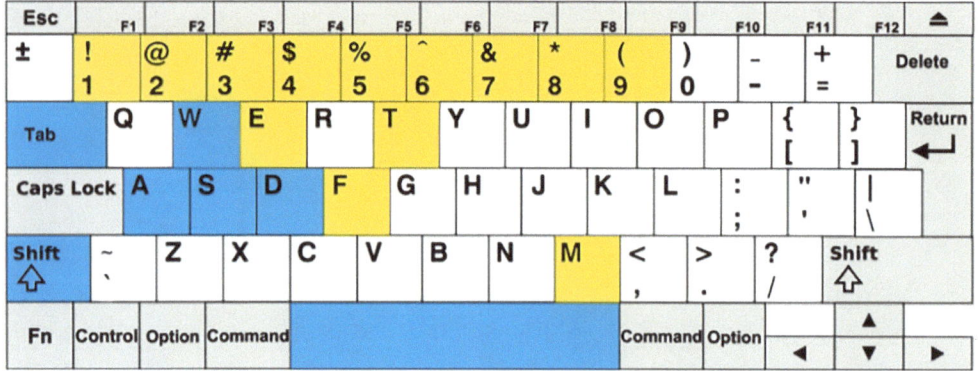

Troubleshooting
Before referring to the debugging steps, check the following:
- Make sure the device connected to WiFi
- Make sure the device is compatible with Vox-L
- Try refreshing the page

Vox-L is running slow:
The most common reason for Vox-L slowing down is too many different entities in the game. Try clearing the world of entities by refreshing the page. Use Ctrl + R. Clearing all entities from the world will allow Vox-L to run at normal performance again.

Cards Won't Scan:
Try loading the card a second time.

Vox-L needs internet connection to load the scripts and assets. If assets from the store and cards aren't loading, it is likely an internet connection problem.

Item is not on hot bar:
When you give yourself an item in Vox-L using either the command blocks or straight from the store, they will not go to the hot bar but instead tot the inventory menu. In order to add the item to the hot bar.

Press the **E** key to open the inventory menu illustrated below. Drag the item to **Slot A** or **Slot B**

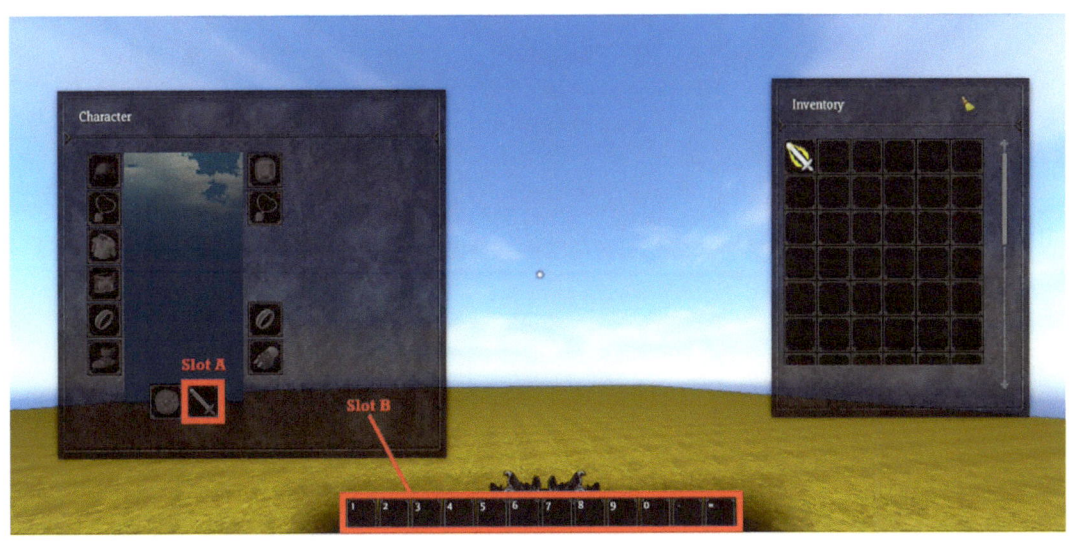

~ Using Vox-L ~

If placed in **Slot A,** the item will be automatically equipped

If placed in **Slot B**, you will have to select the number in which slot it was placed to equip the item. At which point, the item will be moved to **Slot A**

Press the **E** key to close the inventory menu after placing the item in either slot.

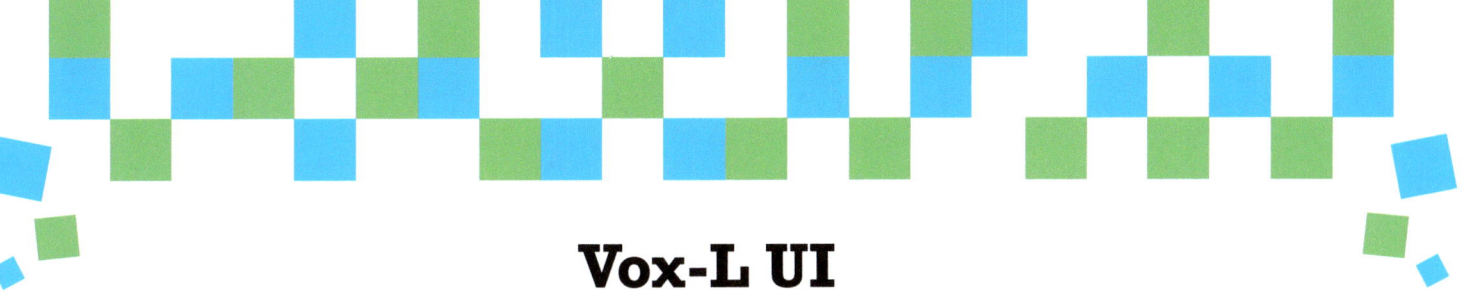

Vox-L UI

Blockly

This is a simple drag-and-drop coding interface that uses blocks that link together to make writing code easier. On the left side of the page there is a list of menus each containing different blockly blocks.

These menus have blocks different blocks inside of them, you can find math operators and number inside the Math category, for loops and while loops in the Loops category, if statements and boolean values in the Logic category, etc. Any block can be dragged of the menu out and be attached to other blocks, like a puzzle piece:

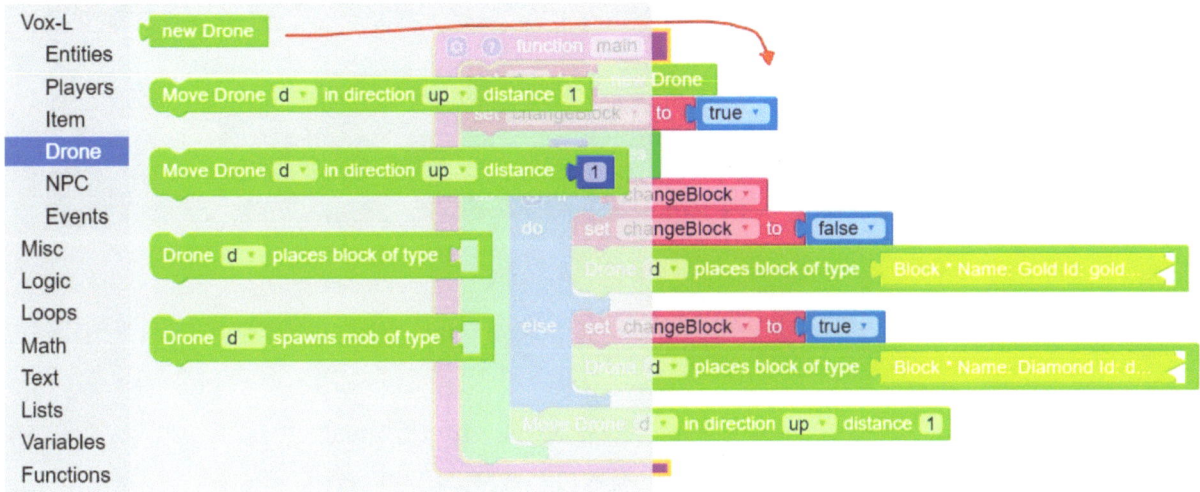

Header Tabs

On the top of the page there are two tabs:

The first one displays the blockly menus and the built blockly code (shown above).

The second one opens the assets library where users can find different looking blocks, items, and characters:

To use them in Vox-L first select a pack and click on it. A small window will open up containing a description of the pack and a button to INSTALL:

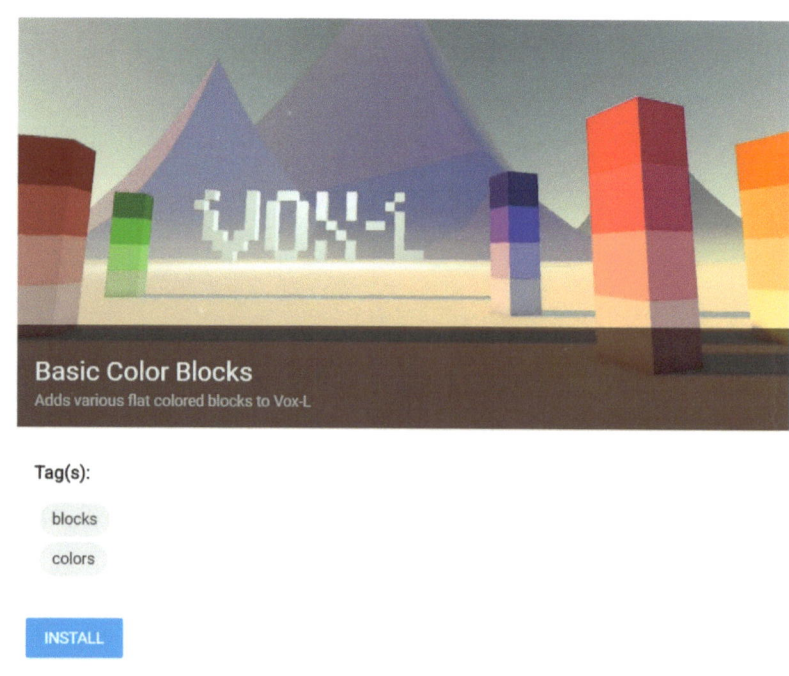

Once you click INSTALL and wait a few seconds the pack will be ready to use. In that same window you can scroll down to view all the new assets that you can select. Assets can either be added to their in-game inventory or get the blockly block to use it in their code:

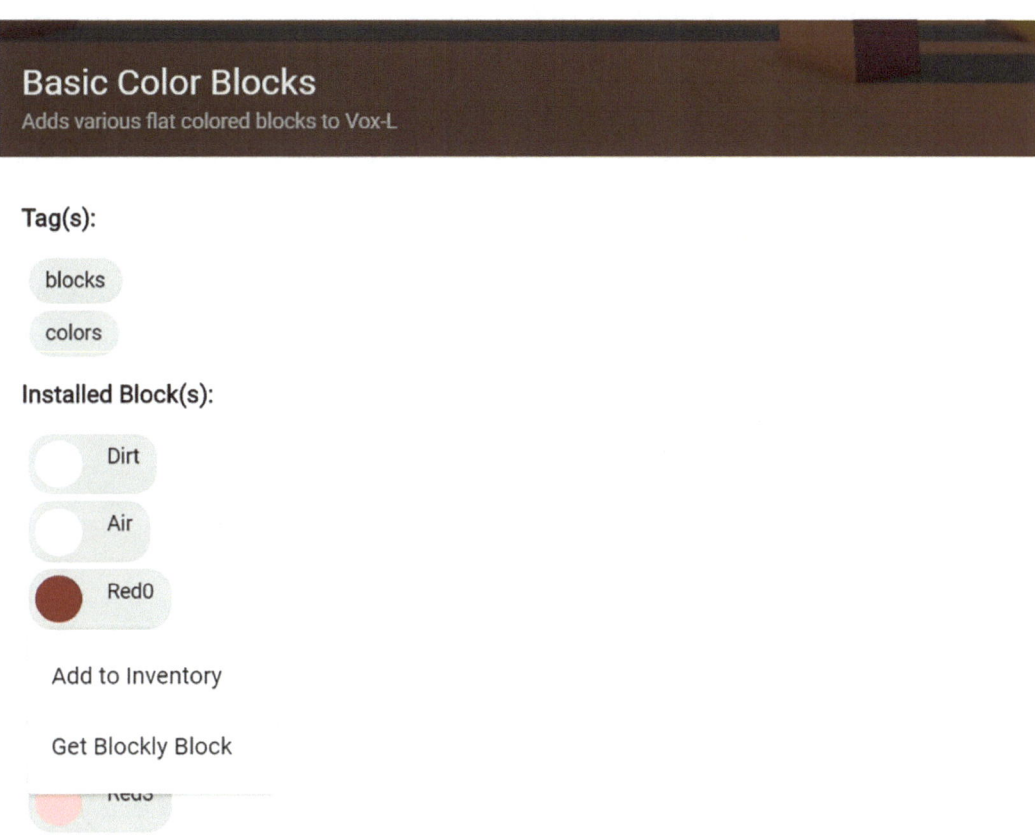

Action Buttons

These are located on the lower left corner. By default only, the Play button appears. To display the other action buttons the user has to hover over the play button and the three other buttons will appear:

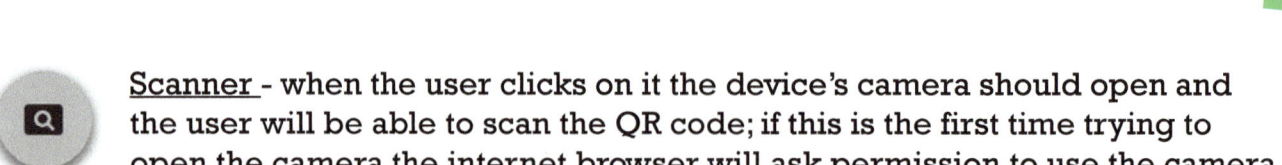

Scanner - when the user clicks on it the device's camera should open and the user will be able to scan the QR code; if this is the first time trying to open the camera the internet browser will ask permission to use the camera.

Downloader - when clicked this will open a small window where you can type in the name of a file. Once the user clicks save, an XML file containing the information of the code currently in the website will be downloaded.

JS generator - when clicked this button will display the generated JavaScript from the blockly code.

Play - when this button is clicked the user will go into the game and the code will execute.

To load an XML file simply drag it into the website.

Scanner
This is used to import pre-built code using a QR code, or to load in a trading card character using the QR code. Once you click on it a small window will open up and it will the display the camera's feed (if this is the first time opening the camera you will need to allow the browser access to it):

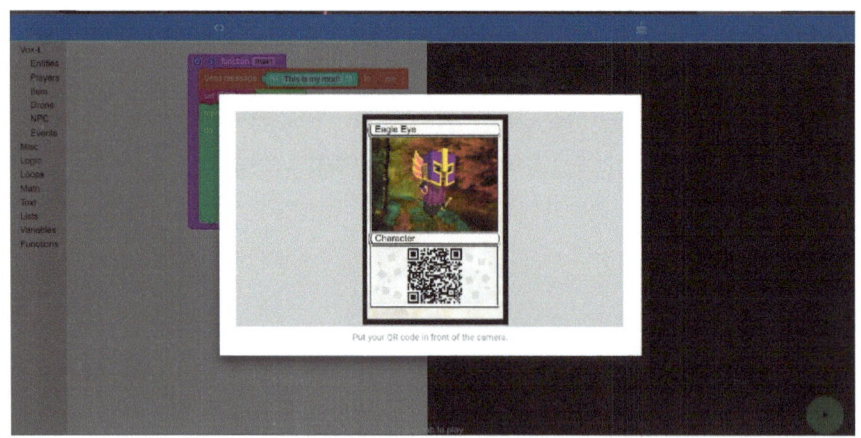

14 ~ Vox-L UI ~

Once the QR is read properly a message will appear asking if you want to load the data or go back to the camera:

If you want to re-load what was scanned simply click on the Scanner button again, and choose LOAD.
If you want to scan something else click the Scanner button and select BACK TO SCAN. That will display the camera's feed again.

Downloader
It is possible to save your mod; either to continue programming later or to share it with someone; by clicking on the Downloader button. When you click this button, a small window will appear asking the user to enter a name for the file. Once the user clicks SAVE it will download an XML file:

To import/load an XML file you can simply drag it into the Vox-L workspace:

~ Vox-L UI ~

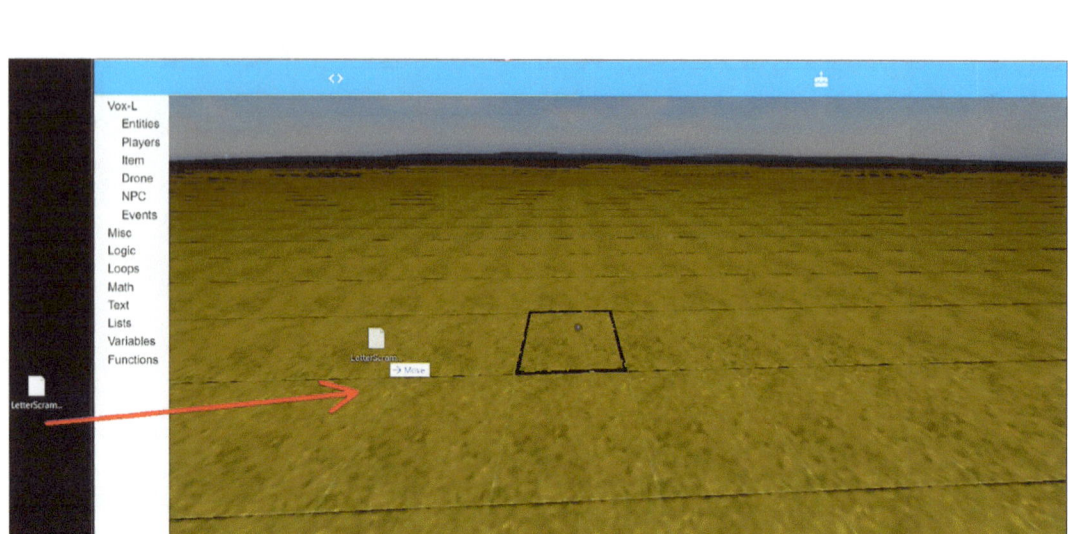

A message confirming the import will appear, select YES.

JS Generator
The JS generator is a great learning tool. Once you click the button it will open a semi-transparent tab on the right side of the workspace. The tab will contain all of the blockly code translated into JavaScript. This is a great way to compare both the blockly and JS to have a better understanding of what the code that is running actually looks like:

~ Vox-L UI ~

Play
This button will run your mod. When the user clicks it the workspace will be replace by the Vox-L world, a 3 second countdown message will be sent and then the mod will run. If this is the very first mod to run in the session, it might take longer than 3 seconds to install any new assets used in the code:

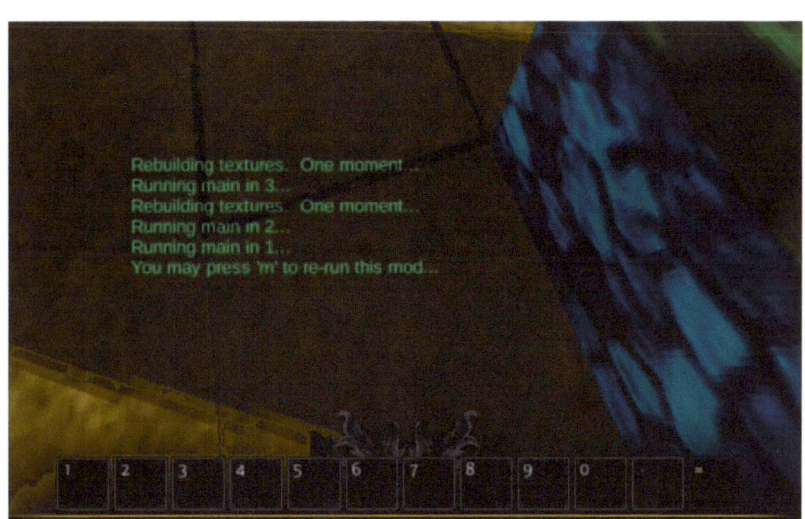

~ Vox-L UI ~

Using the Forum

Forum

This forum is designed for both Vox-L players to discuss things related to Vox-L and for teachers to meet and share teaching techniques. The developers of the game are on the forum, so this is also a great place to discuss bugs and new features. Whether you're talking to the devs or fellow players, remember: Be positive. Be polite. Be friendly.

Creating a New Topic

To create a new class, click the 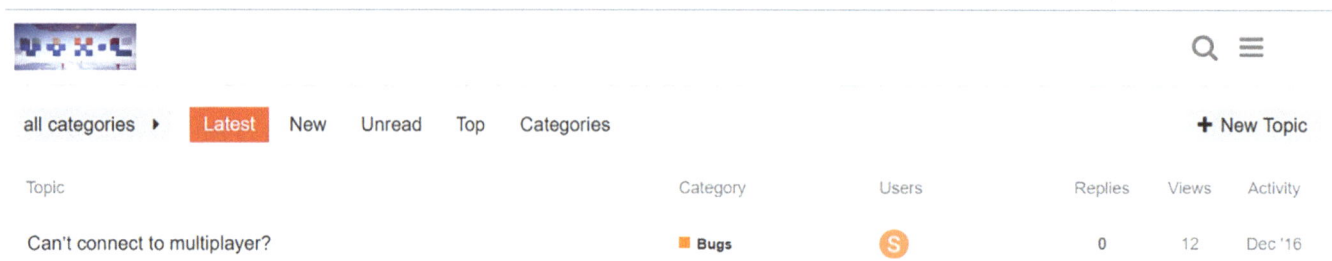 button on the top-right corner. A small window will open on the bottom of the page:

Give your topic a brief description, select a category and start your discussion:

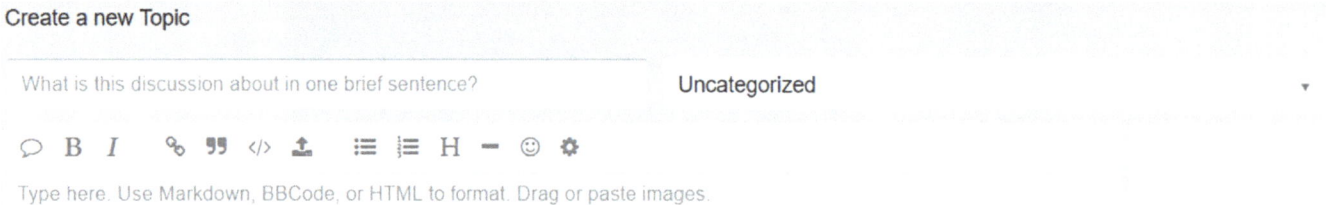

You can have multiple formatting options, the right panel shows what it will look like once it is created. To upload a picture click on the  button, the following will appear:

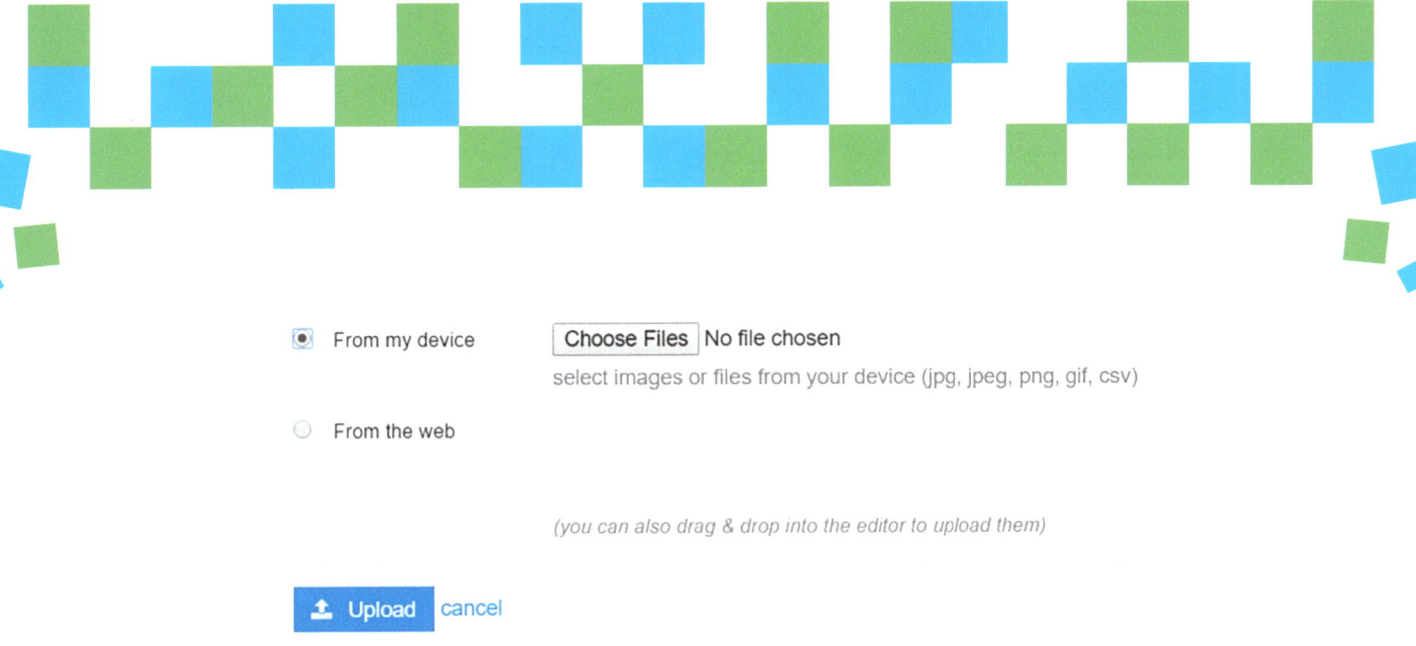

Once you select your file it will upload to the website. The left panel will show the path of the picture, and the right one will show what it will actually look like:

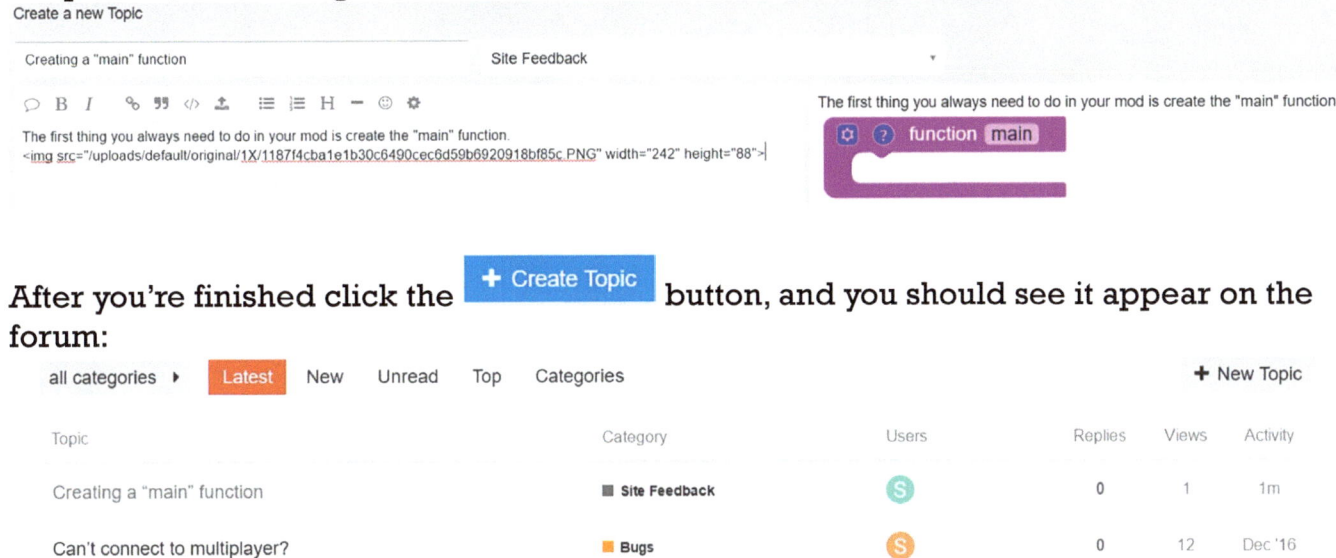

After you're finished click the [+ Create Topic] button, and you should see it appear on the forum:

Contributing to a topic

We encourage users to discuss the forums topics. If you have an answer to a question or simply what to talk about your experience open up a topic and click on the [Reply] button.

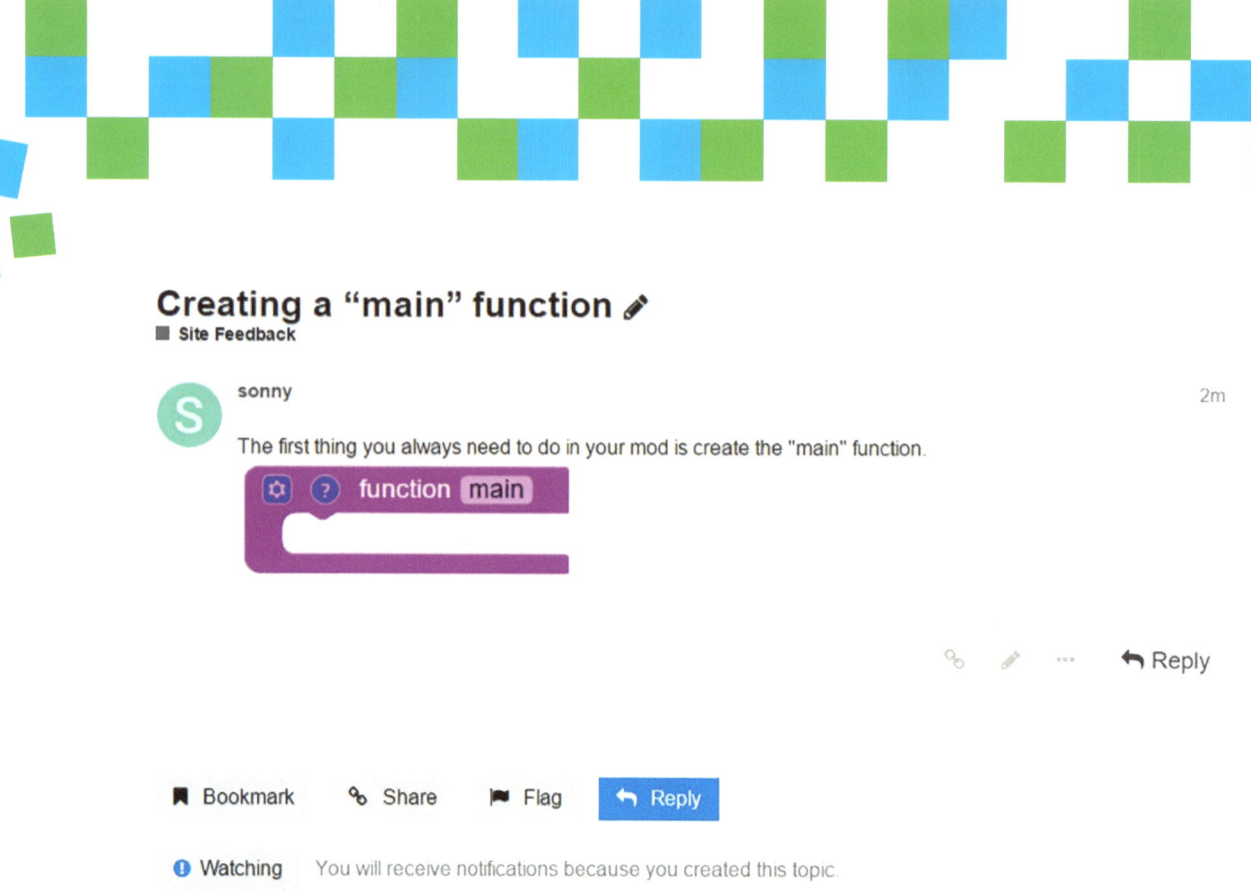

A small window will open up at the bottom of the page where you can add your contribution.

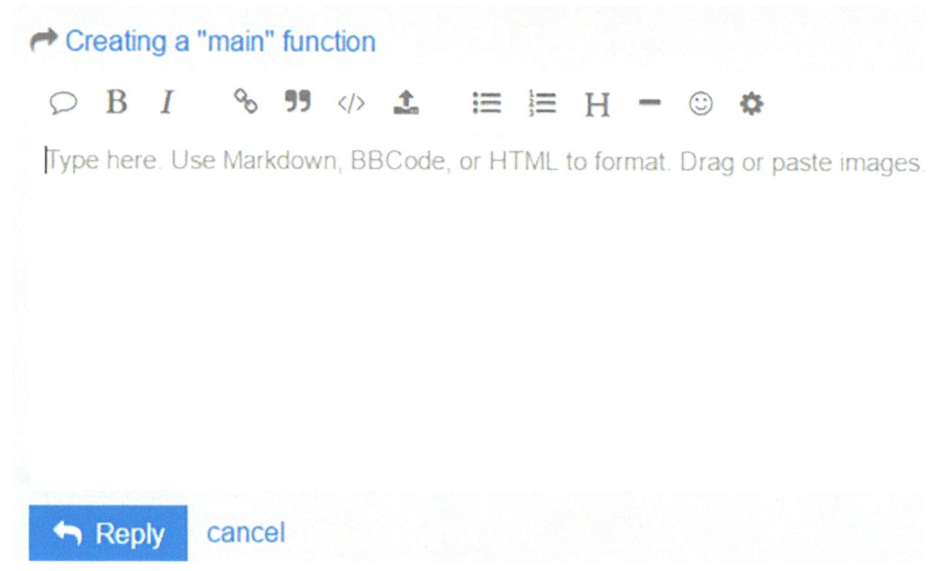

Activities on "/learn"

What is /learn?
/learn refers to the website build.vox-l.com/learn. There you will find several activities for students to work on during class or as extra assignments.

Navigating /learn
When you go to /learn you will see a list of all the concepts: Functions, Loops, Student Resources, etc. At the bottom of each page there is a (Back to Table of Contents) link that will take you back to the home page of /learn.

Choose your Module

- Functions
- Loops
- Parameters
- Logic
- Variables
- Student Resources (Code Examples)

Choose your Activity

- What is a loop?
- Useful loops
- Loop challenge #1
- Loop challenge #2
- Loop challenge #3
- Loop quiz
- Nested loops #1
- Nested loops #2
- Nested loops quiz
- Counter variable loops
- (Back to Table of Contents)

What is a Module?
A module is basically a folder that contains different activities of that specific concept. For example, when you click on the Loops module, it will send you to a page containing several Loops activities. The last module is called "Student Resources (Code Examples.)" In here, you will find small tutorials on how to program simple mods, like controlling entities or adding block break events.

What is an Activity?
When you click on a module it will open up a menu with several activities. These activities are meant to reinforce/review a concept previously taught in class. The majority of these activities have a QR code that can be scanned on the website or a link to download that activity's XML file.

Choose your Media
There are two ways of viewing the activity; via LearnWorlds (online course platform) or a downloadable PDF. The second one opens a PDF file that you can view online or print out. Generally, the first step of this document will instruct the user to scan the QR code to load pre-built code into Vox-L; in the online viewer the user can click on the link to download the same XML file.

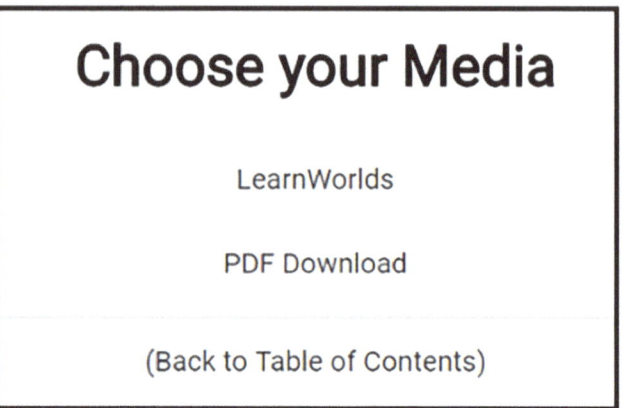

LearnWorlds
LearnWorlds involves the website course.learntomod.com; this is where we host our online courses. Users need to create a (free) account on LearnWorlds to access the activities. Once you create an account and login you will be able to view all of the activities.

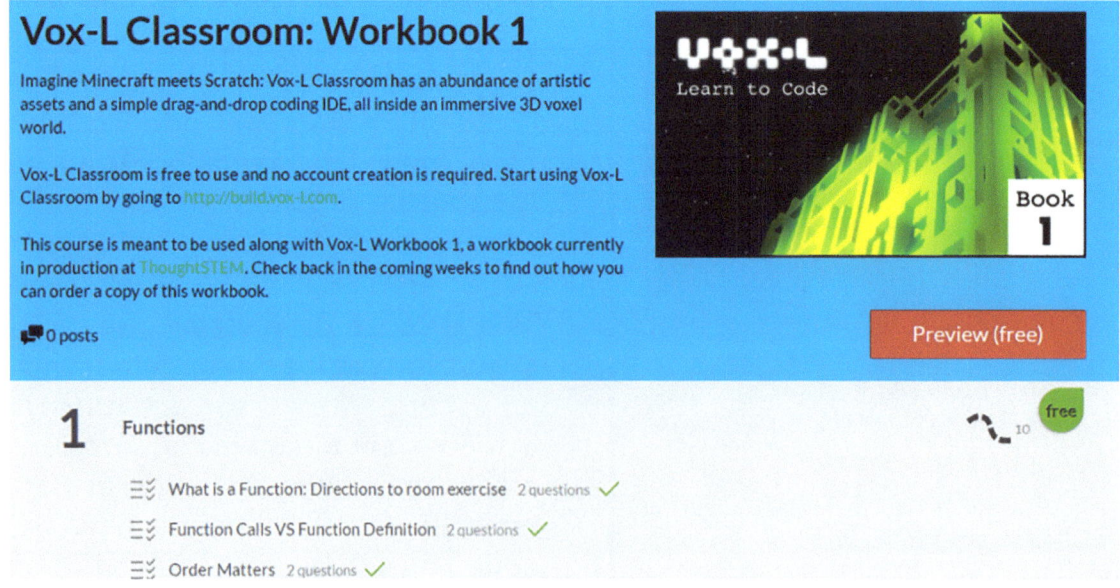

The general structure of these online activities is a short description of the activity followed by steps to modify the given mod. Often the first step will have a link where you can download XML files containing pre-built code that you can load into Vox-L. At the bottom of the activity there's usually an arrow to show the activity's result/answer.

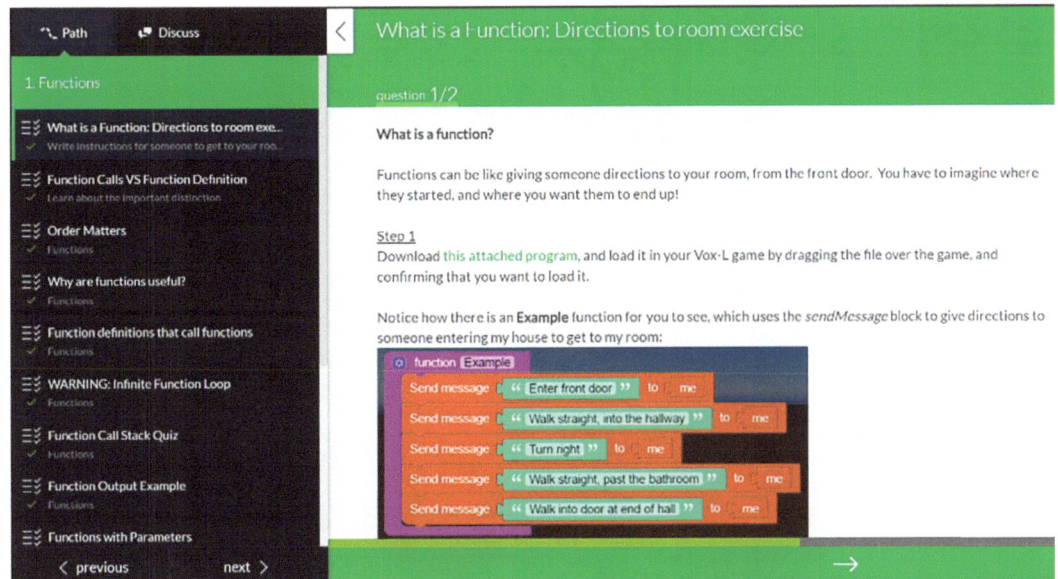

The only difference between the online activity in LearnWorlds and the downloadable PDF is that the instructions and steps in the PDF version were shortened so that the activity could fit in one page.

What is a QR code?
A Quick Response code is a machine-readable code consisting of an array of black and white squares. We use this to store pre-built XML files online. When one of our QR codes is scanned in Vox-L it will automatically load the code associated with it.

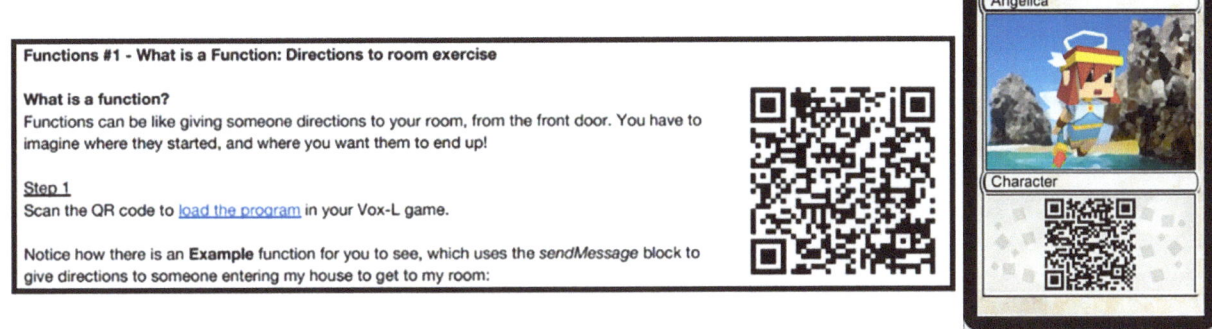

~ Activities on "/learn" ~

What is an XML file?
It stands for Extensible Markup Language. When you want to download your blockly code from Vox-L it will be saved in this type of file, which can then be uploaded or scanned via a QR code.

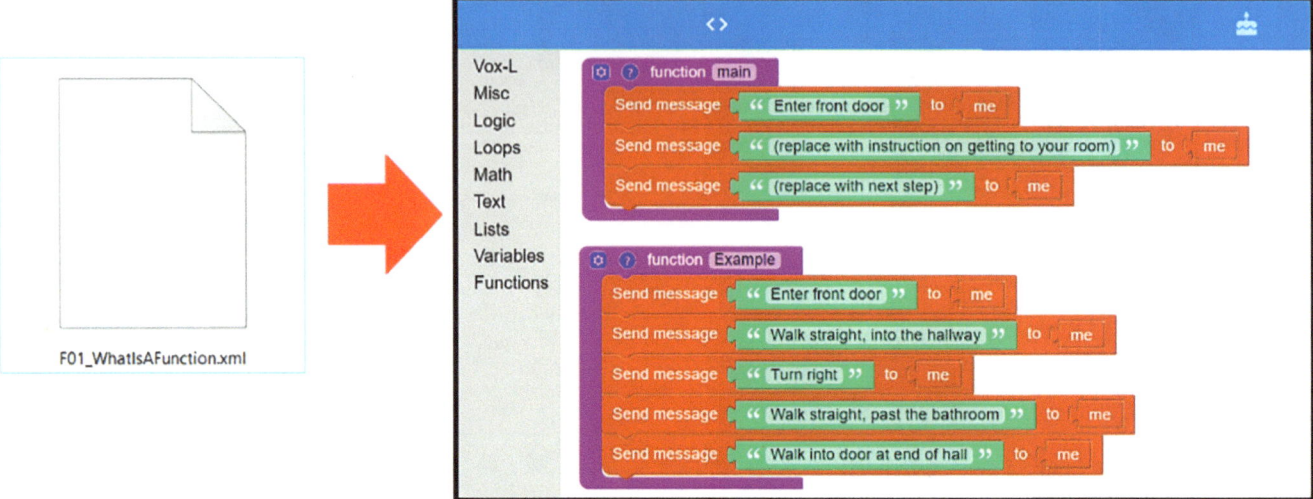

Cards

Special character cards that can be loaded in Vox-L are part of the teacher package. These physical cards have a QR code that can be scanned in Vox-L classroom to load the entity shown on each card. When loaded these entities will behave like ragdolls, nonetheless users can use coding blocks to program them into being NPCs (Non Playable Character). These assets are a great motivator for students and really helpful for artificial intelligence lessons.

Loading Cards to Vox-L
Using the scanner, load the script to place the entity in the world.

Once loaded the entity will float in the world and will only react when the player uses a physical force on them. In order to interact, battle or befriend these creatures, the user must write code for them to do so.

Using them in the classroom
These cards have been used as rewards for participation, completing extra activities, good behavior or as part of an AI lesson. The following code will scan all the entities around a 5 block radius of the player, select the closest one and make it follow the player:

Concepts Explained

This section will give you an overview of the programming concepts that Vox-L and the accompanying curriculum are designed to teach. Throughout this section you will find brief overviews, how the concepts apply in code and helpful discussions to have in class.

Functions

Introduction

Functions are likely to be the very first concept you introduce to your class. No matter what age group you are working with, it is important to understand the infrastructure of code and how computers think before even starting to write code. Computers "think" from top to bottom, and follow specific steps provided. Think of it as reading instructions from a list; if the task is complex enough, one might have multiple lists. Functions would be the list in this analogy. A function contains a process or instructions to a specific topic, these functions can reference other functions using a "function call."

In code

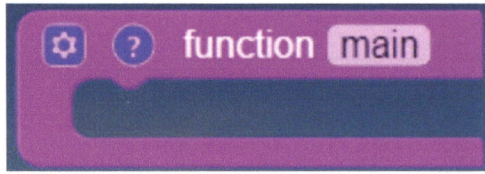

In our mods we always need ONE and ONLY one "main" function, and we have to make sure it's always in lowercase. This is the starting location for our program. If this doesn't exist or it doesn't have anything in it we will get errors when trying to run the mod. Besides our "main" function we can have several other functions that do different things within our mod.

To create a new function we need to first define it. The big purple block that has a mouth is called a "function definition." We can call it whatever we want, but I suggest you give it a meaningful name. For instance if you have a function that gives your player weapons, you can give it a name like "give_weapons," instead of "cool_function." That way in the long run you remember or have an idea what that function does.

If you want to actually use this function in your mod, we have to use a "function call"; which is the small purple block that has the same name as your function definition, in this case "give_weapons," like this:

Therefore when we run this mod we will first get a message, and then we will receive a diamond sword. If you showed somebody the image above and ask them what your mod would do? They could at

26 ~ Concepts Explained ~

least assume that the player would get some type of weapon. This is why using meaningful names is useful, because other people might use it and instead of looking thoroughly at your code they can guess what some functions would do by just looking at the name.

Aid for discussion
When a leading a discussion on functions I make sure to give an example that computers aren't as "smart" as we like to think they are but they are very good at following instructions. When programming we have to make sure to give very clear instructions.

Variables

Introduction
Like in mathematics, physics, or any other science class, we have something called a "Variable." In programming, a variable is a value that can change depending on conditions or information passed to the program.

In code
When we want to use a variable the very first thing we have to do is create that block:

By selecting "Create variable..." we can create a new box; or declare a variable; in the computer. We can have as many variables as we want and they can be of different types, for example: numbers, drones, booleans (true or false), strings (text), or any other value you want to give it:

This only takes care of the first attribute, the name. Now we have to tell the computer what the box is going to contain. Remember to give your variables a meaningful name, that way you or other people can assume what the value of a variable might be.

In this example we have six variables and all of them are of different types. Now whenever we use a variable in our mod, for instance "number," the computer knows what that means; which is "10." Let's say that we are creating a new function to build a tower, we start with something simple and then test this:

~ Concepts Explained ~

27

Aid for Discussion
I like to think that a variable is a box, and that the computer is filled with millions of these very small boxes. Each box has two attributes: the name, and the content. The programmer can choose both of these depending on what the mod needs.

Drones

Introduction

A drone is like an invisible robot that helps you in Vox-L. This drone receives step-by-step instructions that tell it where and how to move. They are very useful when trying to build something, or when trying to spawn mobs at a specific location.

In code
Before using a drone in our mod we have to declare/create it inside a variable. To do this, we go to the "Variables" menu and get the generic variable declaration block:

Then a small window will open in our browser and it will ask us to type in a name. The default name for the drone is simply "d," but you can name it whatever you want.

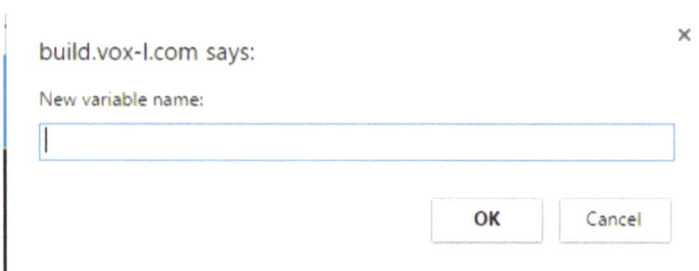

Once we give it a name we have to get our "new Drone" block from the "Drone" menu and attach it inside our variable:

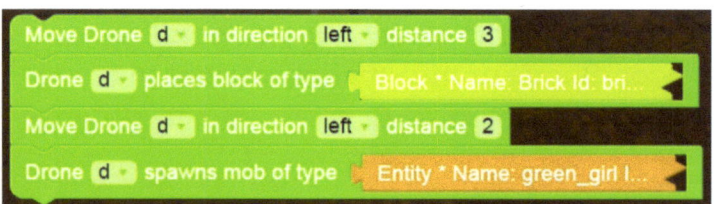

This basically tells the program that whenever we refer to "d," we are talking about our drone. Now we can start using our drone in our program.

These instructions will do the following: move the drone left 3 blocks, place a diamond block, move the drone left 2 blocks, spawn a green girl.

Common Errors
The most common mistake is when the programmer creates a variable with some name "drone1," but then when it gets used the default name "d" is not changed:

This will produce an error, because in this cause the program does not know what "d" is; therefore we need to change that to "drone1" since we said that was the name of our drone.

Another common problem has to do with what level the drone builds its blocks on. By default, it will place blocks or entities starting at the block you're looking at, or at the same location as the player.

Using code that looks something like this (truncated for length):

When the code runs the drone would build the structure at ground level, like this:

Which is probably not what your animals want. To fix this, all you need to do is add this block, to the spot right before where your drone places its first block, like this:

Now, when you run it it should do this:

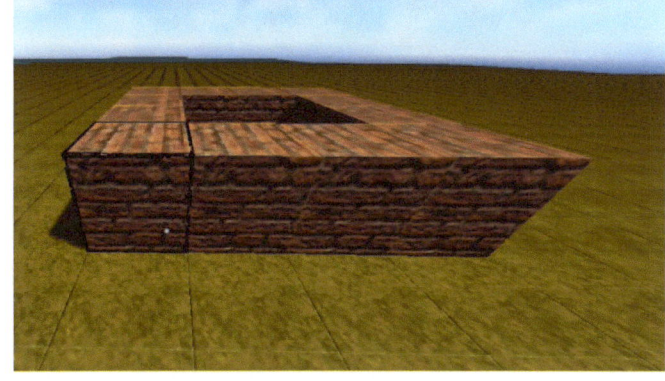

Yay, the enclosure is above-ground!

~ Concepts Explained ~

Aid for Discussion
A Drone can be thought as a robot that follows simple instructions like move, place or summon. In class you can act like the robot and follow instructions, like the game Simon says, in order to help them understand that they need to be precise in their instructions.

Materials

Introduction

In order to summon or get materials in Vox-L, you must enter the asset store. You can enter the asset store by clicking on the cake tab, found in the coding overlay.

After entering this menu, you will see a list of possible assets that can be added to the Vox-L world. Select an asset by clicking on the image.

After clicking on the image, you will have to install the asset. Click the blue install button located at the bottom of the page. You will need internet connection for this.

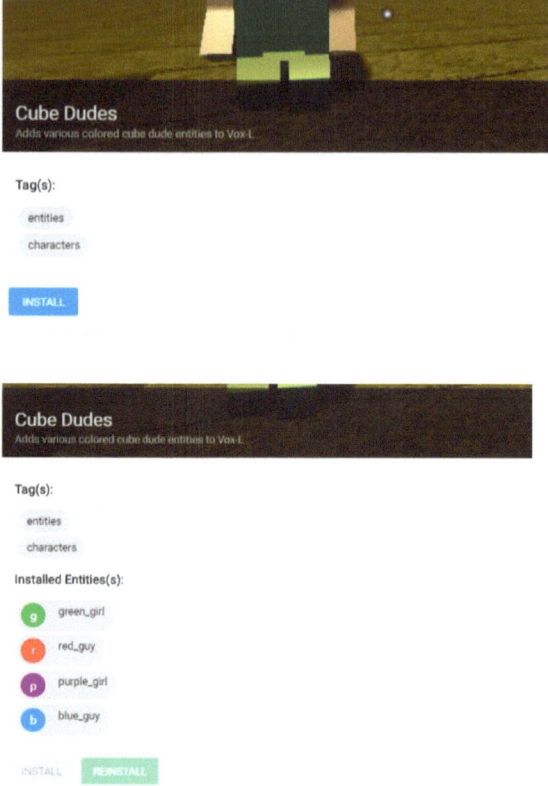

Once the asset has been installed, you will see a list of the installed entities, items or blocks. By clicking on those items, you will see options to either place them in game, or to get a blockly block for them.

Placing them in Vox-L will close the coding menu, getting a blockly block will allow you to write code or make a mod with the selected asset. This process is needed for placing blocks or entities when using drones.

30   ~ Concepts Explained ~

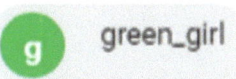

Summon In Game

Get Blockly Block

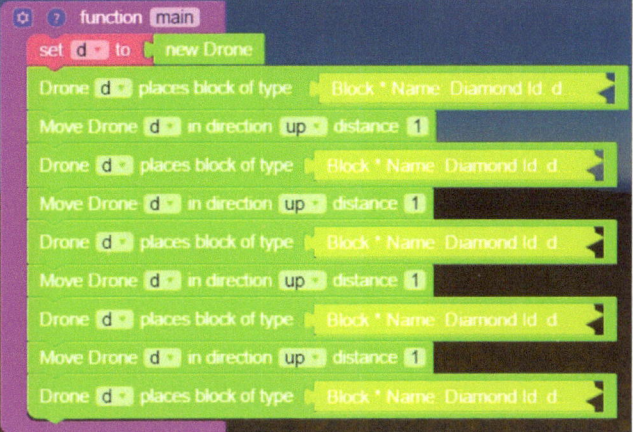

Loops

Introduction

Loops are a very helpful tool for programmers. It helps us repeat a set of instructions and keeps code short. The code that gets placed inside a loop block will be repeated a certain number of times. This will make our code compact and clear.

In code

Let's say we want to build a tower of blocks 5 high. Our code might look something like this:

If we wanted to change that tower to be 100 blocks high, not only would it take a long time to program but it would also make a very long script. Let's change our code to use a loop instead. It'll look as follows:

Now, if we want to make the tower 100 blocks high again, all we would need is to change one number:

Common Errors

It is important to remember that the all of the code placed inside the loops will be repeated, this means we have to be wise when choosing what code to place inside the loop and what to leave out. As an instructor, you will most likely than not see

~ Concepts Explained ~

the following code:

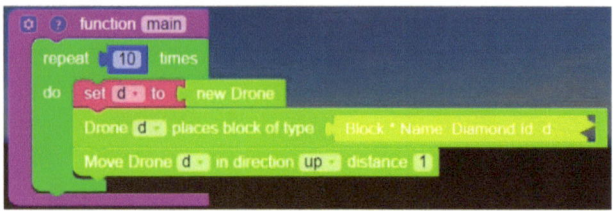

What exactly is wrong with this code? The problem is that the drone is inside the loop. This means that the drone will never get a chance to create a tower since it is constantly recreated. A drone is always created at the location the player is looking at. Here is the sequence the code goes through:

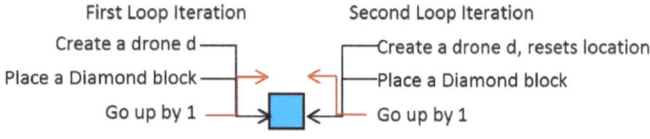

Aid for Discussion
Loops can be thought as daily routines. For example students during the weekday always wake up, get ready, have breakfast, go to school, have lunch, go back home, do homework, sleep.

Parameters

Introduction
A function can be given extra values when it gets called, these values are called parameters, and they are stored in variables. Let's imagine a student wants to simply send a message to a user, the code for it would look something like this:

This code could be rearranged so that the message is in a separate function. Usually a message is followed with some other code. Therefore when we move the message to a new function more code could be added to that function and not clutter up the main function:

Now, what if we want to send two messages in two separate functions? We could simply create two functions with their own messages:

What if we want to send three messages, or five, or ten? It would start to become redundant to keep creating one function for each message. That's where Functions with Parameters come in.

In code
Instead of calling different functions with their own message. We could simply create one function called "say_something" and give it an input.

On the "say_something" function click on the blue cog and a small window should appear. In that window drag the "input name:" block to the right side and put it inside of "inputs." Instead of the "x," give it a meaningful name like "text." Now whenever you call the "say_something" function you can give it an input, in this case a piece of text. Then we can use that input that is stored in the variable "text," inside if our function and sent a message with that.

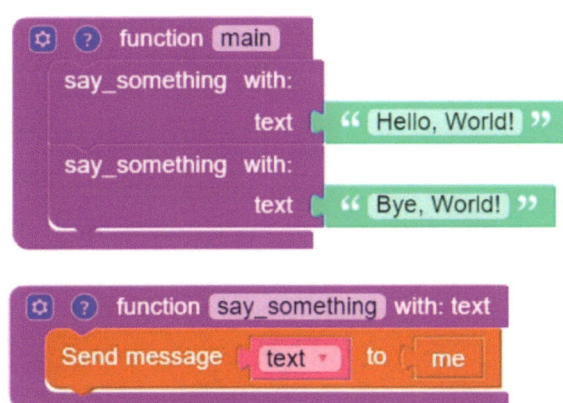

Aid for Discussion
You can use daily action as an example. People eat, dress up, drive places, watch tv, and all of these can be examples of functions. The parameters would be the specific parts of that actions, eating pizza, putting on a suit, driving to the mall, watching cartoons.

Logic Statements

These statements are basically a set of evaluations. Usually a value of something, that is stored in a variable, goes through a series of checks that compare the variable to an arbitrary value. These comparisons happen in order, and the first one to be evaluated to true will be the one to execute.

In Code
Let's say we want to evaluate a number and determine if it's odd or even. Since we know even numbers are evenly divisible by 2 we can use this as our evaluation. You can follow these steps:

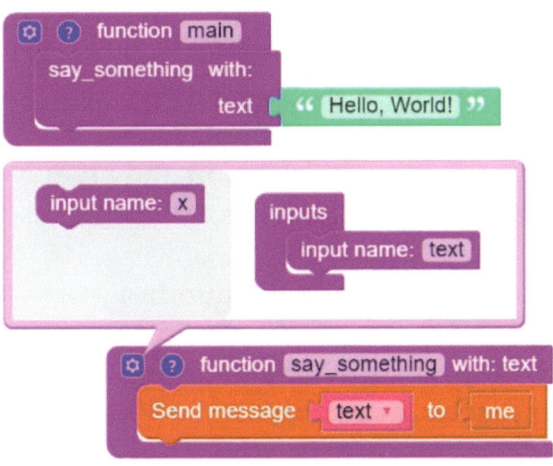

With this simple change, we can call our function as many times as we want, and just change the parameter; the message; to send out different messages:

~ Concepts Explained ~

Create a "main" function, and a "number" variable with any value

Get the logical statement. It automatically contains an "If," to add an "else" click on the blue cog and drag an "else" block into the right side

Once you have this setup we can now add the evaluation. We said that an even number is evenly divisible by two, meaning there is no remainder. Under the "Math" menu there is a block that says "remainder of blank ÷ blank." In the first blank we should add our variable "number" and in the second one we can place a number "2"

After that we can create an output message according to the result of the evaluation

With this final mod, we can logically check if a number is even or odd. The value of the "number" variable can be changed to another number to see how the behavior changes.

As stated before, logical statements evaluate values in order (top to bottom) and they stop in the first check that equates to "true." In the previous example we only had one evaluation, but there can be more than one; this is where the "else if" comes in. When a student wants to implement more than one logical calculation, they can add as many "else if" blocks as they want.

Imagine we want to check if a number is divisible by 2, 3, 5, or 7. We could add more checks to our previous mod and have something that looks like this:

~ Concepts Explained ~

Remember that the statement will stop whenever one expression evaluates to "true." Even though the number "35" is a multiple of "5" and "7," we first check if "35" is a multiple of "5" which evaluates to true therefore it stops and outputs the message "This number is a multiple of 5."

Aid for Discussion
You can think of logic comparisons as being true or false questions. Whatever you are comparing can only be either right or wrong.

Events

In Vox-L there are a few different events that happen in the game and we might not be aware of them. The game registers events as we play, some examples are "block_break," "player_chat" or "block_place." The Vox-L software already has these events hard coded into the event block:

To create a simple mod that uses an event we would need to create something like this:

In this code the aqua block is telling the computer to run the function "message" when a block is broken. The black block is called a "function reference," and like the name says it refers to a function that will run whenever some event happens. According to this code, when we run the mod the computer will write a note in its memory that says "Whenever a block breaks I will run the 'message' function." Then when the player breaks a block it will run the "message" function and simply output the message.

In code
Whenever an event is registered in Vox-L, there's extra information that is attached to that event. For instance, when we break a block the computer registers that event and also retrieves information such as: the

~ Concepts Explained ~

35

type of block, the location of it, who broke it, etc.

Using Functions with Parameters we can retrieve the information of these events. Let's say we want to know the type of block that was broken. These would be the steps to set that up:

Create the "main" function with a "block_break" event referencing the "onBreak" function; also add the "info" parameter

Using the "info" parameter we can retrieve the block that was broken. First we create JS block with "info.old_material"

After that simply send a message with the value of broken_block

With this mod every time the player breaks a block a message will be sent with the material of that block:

This is only one example using the "block_break" event, but this could be done similarly with other events like "player_chat" or "block_place."

Aid for Discussion
You can think of events action and the functions they call as the reaction. An everyday event can be whenever you get thirsty you need to drink water, or whenever you feel tired you need to sleep.

Events with Logic Statements

Introduction
Once students learn and understand logic statements and events they will be ready to combine the two concepts and create more complex code.

These two concepts are very useful when you want your code to act different depending on what's happening in Vox-L. For example, imagine your mod has a block break event and it gives you a sword every time you break any block. That's cool, but it would be better if you had to break a specific block to get the sword.

In code
Once you create a mod that uses a block break event and sends a message with the name of that block, it's very easy to add the logical statement.

~ Concepts Explained ~

[code blocks image]

After the message block add an if statement and compare the value of the broken_block variable with a text block containing the name of the block:

[code blocks image]

Now, only when you break a diamond block you will get the interior message. That's not very exciting so instead you can give the player a diamond sword. Besides that you can add more comparison, that way whenever you break other blocks other special things will happen:

[code blocks image]

Aid for Discussion
Using the Events example of actions and reactions you can now have more than one option. For example, when you get tired and it's during the day you can take a nap, if it's during the evening you can just go to sleep until the next day.

Workbook Answers

Section 1 - Intro Activities

Trickster Code

Circle:

Print.("Hi")

[Send: "Hi" block]

Square:

console.Log("Have a great day.")
console.Log("Have a great day.")

Riddle Me a Riddle

1. P - since 5 >= 4, print P
2. T - since 5 X 3 = 15 and we're looking for a triangle, select T
3. A - since 5 is not even, print A
4. Y - since 5 = 5, print Y

The daughter's name is PATTY

Function Teams

If coin's value is 25 cents:
    collect
otherwise:
    move on to next coin

[Send: "Quarter" block]

Translating

1. This piece of code will display the text "message" in a console for the user to see.
2. This piece of code will grab a coin, check the value of it, if the value is 25 it will be placed in a bin, if it is not 25 it will grab the next coin and check again.

Section 2 - Functions

Potion Makin'

Strength Potion	
(Teacher's Notes)	(My notes)
Put in 1 Barbell	Put in 1 Barbell
Put in 2 cups of Whey Powder	Put in 2 (pounds) of Whey Powder
Repeat 2x	Repeat 2x
Turn right twice	Turn (left) twice
Turn left twice	Turn (right) twice
Wring Sweaty Towel over Cauldron	Wring Sweaty Towel over Cauldron
Let sit for 45 minutes	Let sit for (35) minutes

Answers

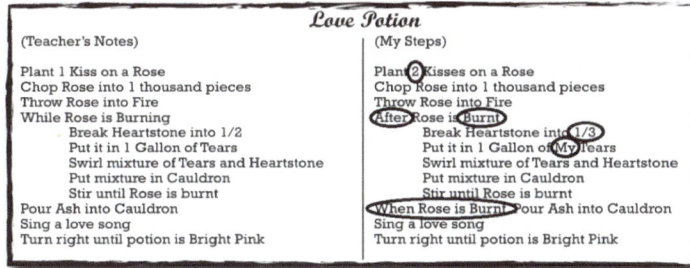

Shape Collector

1. Function 1: collect Star
2. Function 3: collect Hexagon
3. Function 2: collect Triangle
4. Function 4: collect Circle

Name That Function!

- "moveUP" - C
- "placeTNT" - A
- "moveRight" - D
- "placeDirt" - F
- "moveLeft" - E
- "spawnCow" - B

Passing In With Parameters

Variable Cake
- Message sent is: 8
- Message sent is: 4

Variable size and color
- Shirts bought: small blue shirt, large blue shirt
- Shirts bought: 2 large red shirts

Variable Name
- Mark will buy apples
- Alex will buy milk
- Mark will buy apples

Hanging with Jillian

1. The tower is 2 books high
2. Score
3. The value of z is 2
4. She did not draw a square

Family Reunion

1. Yes
2. No
3. Yes
4. No
5. Erik son of Carlos will listen, but not Erik the son of Haley

Potion Makin': Midterm Time

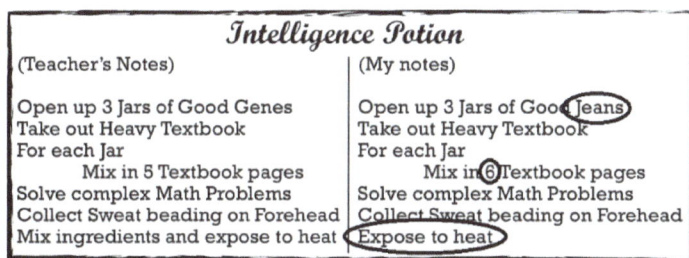

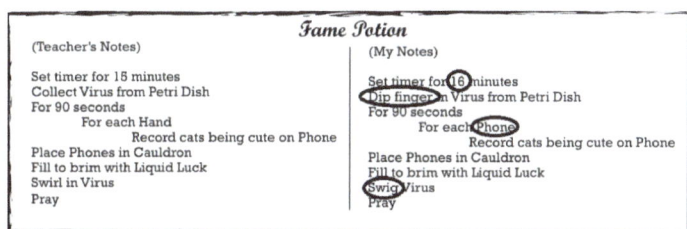

Name That Function

- "goNowhere" - A
- "volcano" - B
- "goldenCreeper" - D
- "creeperSwarm" - F
- "moveDiagonallyUp" - E
- "waterWell" - C

~WorkbookAnswers~   39

Answers

Passing In With Parameters

Variable pizza
- Message sent is: "more please"
- Message sent is: "full"

Variable power and name
- Message sent is: : "Oscar the Wizard"
- Message sent is: "Lucy The Fastest"

Variable Name
- When "venom:" the message "potion not allowed" will be sent
- When "speed:" the player will become faster
- When "ACID:" the message "potion not allowed" will be sent (because of capitalization)

Family Reunion

1. No
2. Yes
3. Yes
4. Yes
5. No

Hanging with Jillian 2.0

1. 20 gallons X 200 miles/gallon = 4,000 miles
2. No - cookies were not placed in cart
3. No - user only gathered the ingredients, did not make a sandwich
4. No - blocks were never placed

Section 3 - Variables

Find the Correct Lockers!

- Lunchbox --> Sammy
- Microscope --> Lab Supplies
- Projector --> Mr. Smith
- Football --> Coach Calhoon
- Atendance Sheet --> Mr. Smith
- Mop --> Cleaning Supplies
- Homework --> Sammy
- White Coat --> Lab Supplies

Room Swap

1. Uncle Carlos swap with Carl
2. Shelly swap with Dad
3. Dad swap with Aunt Jane

Tie the Type!

- Repeat 10 times --> Loop
- Block_Break --> Event
- "summonSeep" --> Command
- + --> Operation
- = --> Comparator
- Info --> Parameter

Find the Variables

a. We plan on arriving at the (park) at (4pm)
b. We plan on arriving at the (baseball field) at (7pm)
c. We plan on arriving at the movies at 3pm.
d. We plan on arriving at the house at 10pm.

a. Before you can (go to Shelly's house) you must (clean your room)
b. Before you can (play videogames) you must (do the dishes)
c. Before you can go to bed you must brush your teeth.
d. Before you can go to the party you must finish your homework.

Values and Variables

- "One" --> String
- 1 --> Number
- false --> Boolean
- 1, 2, 3, --> List
- main() --> Function
- me --> Player

Answers

Room Swap 2

1. Swap Carl and Uncle Carlos
2. Swap Phil and Aunt Jane
3. Swap Mom and Carl
4. Swap Dad and Phil
5. Swap Aunt Jane and Mom
6. Swap Shelly and Mom
7. Swap Dad and Shelly
8. Swap Shelly and Uncle Carlos (even though Uncle Carlos and Aunt Jane are not in the same position they're still in the same room)

Values and Variables

- Message sent: "morning"
- Message sent: "16"
- Message sent: "20"
- The code will summon 2 Pigs

Find the Correct Lockers

- Graded tests --> Mr. Smith
- Basketball --> Coach Calhoon
- Trash Bags --> Cleaning Supplies
- Teacher Manual --> Mr. Smith
- Backpack --> Sammy
- Satefly Glasses --> Lab Supplies
- Broom --> Cleaning Supplies
- Weights --> Coach Calhoon

Riddle Me a Riddle

1. I went to the store today and bought an elephant for $10.00
2. My house has 16 bedrooms and 2 bathrooms.
3. Every year around Halloween time, my family and I go to the cemetary, where they have ice cream
4. At the park, my favorite birds to see are flamingos

Section 4 - Loops

Gather the Livestock

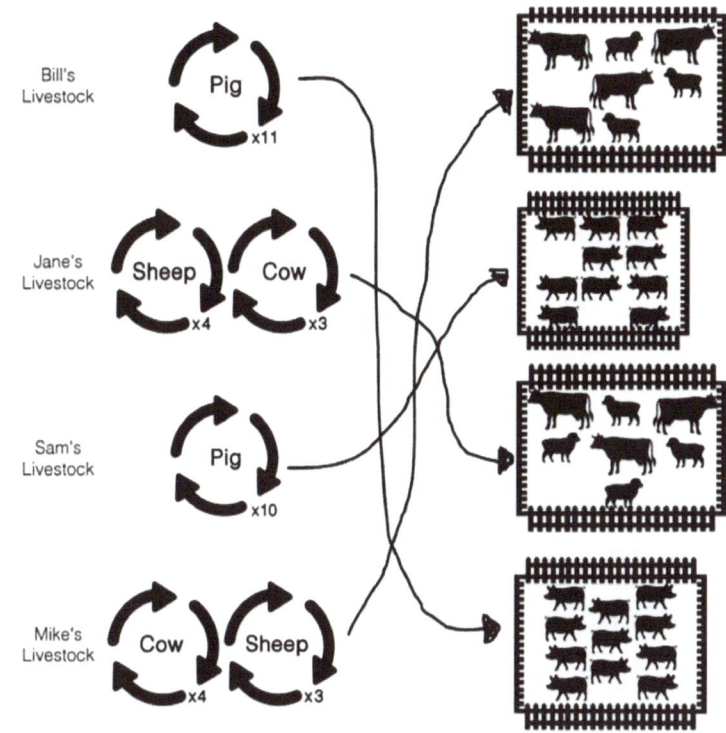

Buying Livestock

- Buy Cow x 4, Buy Pig x 5
- Buy Pig x 10, Buy Sheep x 2
- Buy Cow x 3, Buy Pig x 3, Buy Sheep x 3
- Buy Cow x 2, Buy Pig x 6, Buy Sheep x 1

Lunch Time

- Order Pizza x 3
- Order Banana x 2
- Order Cake x 2
- Order Hamburger x 2
- Order Apple x 3
- Coffee x 2
- Order Water x 4

Answers

Fill in the Squares

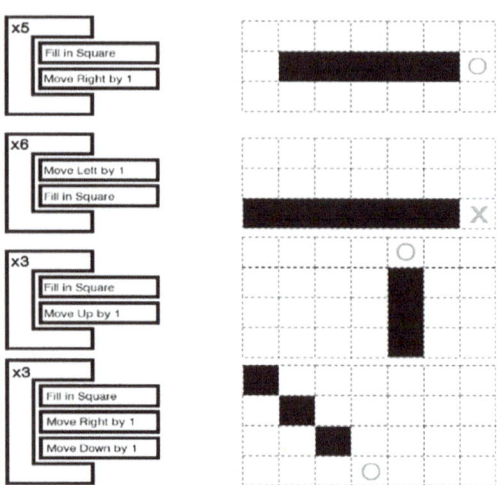

Draw the Structure

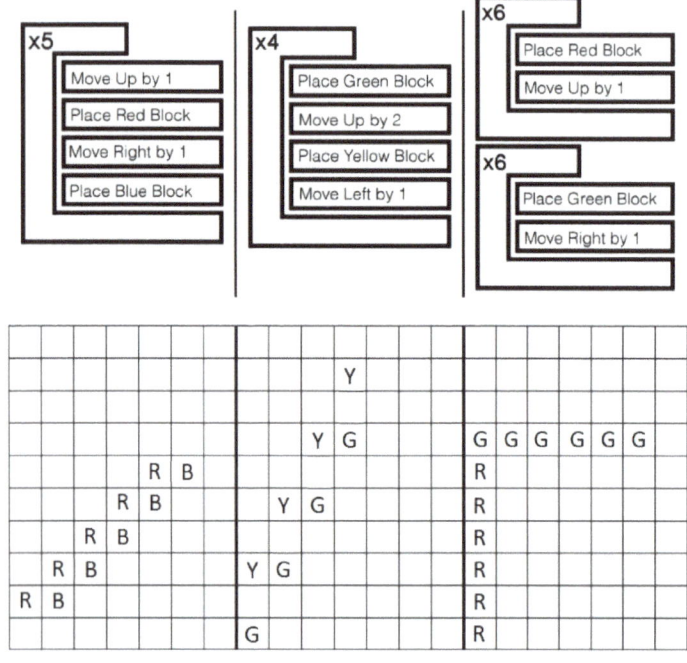

Write the Code

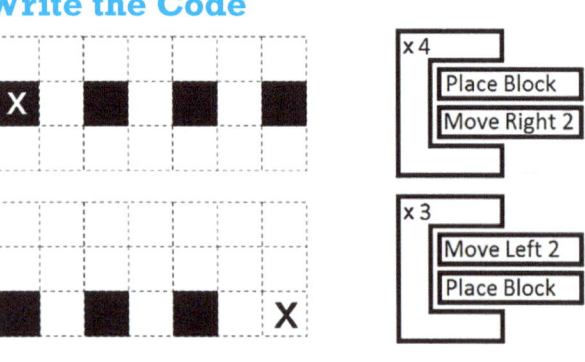

Draw the Structure 2.0

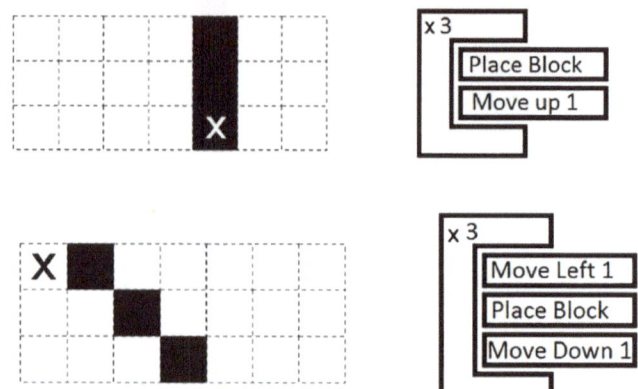

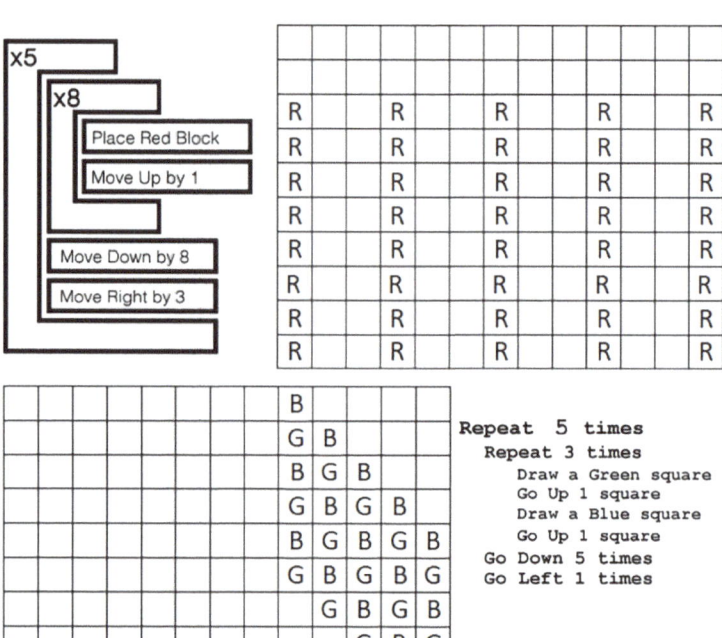

Dinner Time

table_list =
- Fork
- Glass
- Plate
- Coffee Mug
- Knife
- Spoon

Repeat 6 times

42

~WorkbookAnswers~

Answers

Loop The List

set task_list to:
- Wake Up
- Get Ready
- Go School
- Go Home
- Do Homework
- Sleep

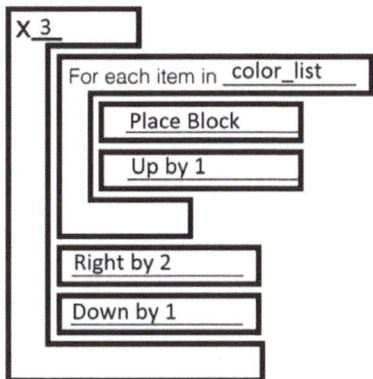

Counter Loops

5, 7, 9, 11
5, 8, 11, 14, 17, 20, 23, 26, 29, 32
Draw the structure resulting from this code:

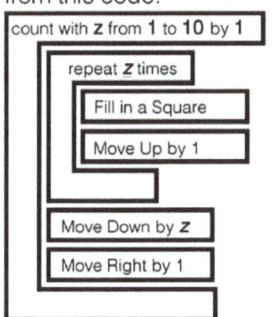 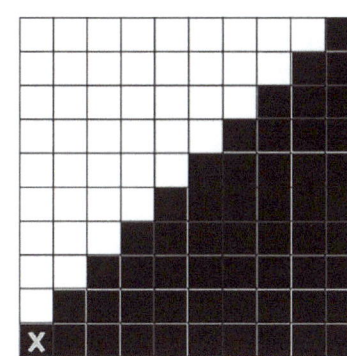

Section 5 - Parameters

Help the Miners

- #1: num = 2, item = bottles of water
- #2: num = 2, item = pickaxes
- #3: num = 2, item = hammers; num = 3, item = shovels
- #4: num = 5, item = chisels; num = 2, item = pickaxes; num = 3, item = lightbulbs

Ordering Food

Table 1
- Sandwich (beef, 2)
- Sandwich (chicken, 1)
- Drink (iced tea, 1)
- Drink (soda, 2)

Table 2
- Sandwich (chicken, 2)
- Sandwich (fish, 1)
- Drink (water, 2)
- Drink (iced tea, 1)

Table 3
- Sandwich (fish, 1)
- Sandwich (beef, 1)
- Drink (soda, 2)

Color Towers

Building 1
- Tower (red, 4)

Building 2
- Tower (blue, 7)

Building 1
- Tower (green, 2)

Building 1
- Tower (yellow, 4)

Go With The Flow

- #1: Ribbon
- #2: Medal
- #3: Medal
- #4: Ribbon

Answers

- #5: Certificate
- #6: Medal

Calorie Counting

- energy = 5
- energy = 42
- calculate(bread, 5, 7)
- calculate(chocolate, 5, 29)
- No, energy = 72
- Yes
- No, energy = 13

Pizza Delivery

1. num = 1, size = extra large, type = pepperoni
2. num = 2, size = medium, type = hawaiian
3. num = 2, size = small, type = cheese
4. num = 2, size = large, type = pepperoni; num = 1, size = medium, type = supreme.

Pizza Delivery

1. Container: bowl, scoops: 2, flavor: vanilla, toppings: chocolate syrup
2. Container: sugar cone, scoops: 3, flavo: vanilla, toppings: bananas
3. Container: waffle cone, scoops: 1, flavor: vanilla, toppings: fresh strawberries.
4. Container: cup, scoops: 4:, flavor: cookies and cream, toppings: chocolate chips

Packing Fruit

Order 1
1. Box A: (apple, 3)
2. Box B: (banana, 4)
3. Box C: (grapes, 2)
4. Box D: (pear, 3)
5. Box E: (pineapple, 4)

Order #2
1. box A: (apple, 3)
2. box B: (banana, 2)
3. box C: (grapes, 5)
4. box D: (pear, 3)
5. box E: (pineapple, 4)

Follow the Food

1. Sandwich
2. Burger
3. Cereal
4. Pizza
5. Sandwich
6. Spaghetti

Packing Fruit

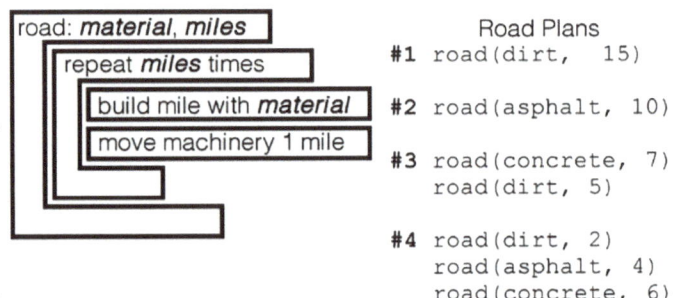

#1	D	D	D	D	D	D	D	D	D	D	D	D	D	
#2	A	A	A	A	A	A	A	A	A					
#3	C	C	C	C	C	C	D	D	D	D				
#4	D	D	A	A	A	C	C	C	C	C	C			

Section 6 - Logic

Lucky Meal Plan

- Bill is more likely to eat Pizza
- Bill is least likely to eat Salad
- Variables: dieRoll, coinFlip
- False, water and soda are equally likely to

Answers

be selected
- True, dieRoll is from 1 to 6

Unscramble

- INITIALIZING
- FUNCTIONS
- CONDITION
- ELSE

Grandma's Grocery List

- Apple
- Strawberry, Mango, Banana
- Move on to next item
- No, adding the items in the list the maximum number she could get is 10
- If it is a fruit

Lucky Meal Plan

```
pick up item
set apple_count to 0
set orange_count to 0

if item is vegetable
        go to next item
else if item is  fruit
        check fruitType
                if fruitType is  apple
                        put 3 of item in cart
                        set apple_count to  3
                if fruitType is  orange
                        put  5  of item in cart
                        set  orange_count  to   5
                if apple_count + orange_count equals   8
                        go to register
                else
                        go to next item
```

Safety First

```
Init Phase 1
Init Entry blank

If Phase = 1
        If Entry = Yellow
                Add 1 to Phase
        Else
                Reset Phase
If Phase = 2
        If Entry = Red
                Add 1 to Phase
        Else
                Reset Phase
If Phase = 3
        If Entry = Blue
                Add 1 to Phase
        Else
                Reset Phase
If Phase = 4
        If Entry = Green
                Print "You got it!"
                Unlock
        Else
                Reset Phase
```

Spare Change

Pick up item
    Is it a coin?
        If the value is 25
            name it "Quarter"
        If the value is 10
            name it "Dime"
        If the value is 5
            name it "Nickel"
        If the value is 1
            name it "Penny"

Missing Numbers

1. 2, 4, 8, 16, 32, 64 -- previous number times 2
2. triangle, square, circle, square, triangle, square, circle
3. 2, 5, 11, 23, 47, 95 -- previous number

Answers

times 2 plus 1
4. 7, 12, 17, 22, 27, 32
5. 9, 16, 23, 30, 37 -- previous number plus 7
6. blue, red, blue, red, green, blue, red, blue, red, green
7. 3, 6, 12, 24, 48 -- previous number times 2

Tic-Tac-Toe

- In a corner 75% of winning, center only has 50%
- No, corner or center

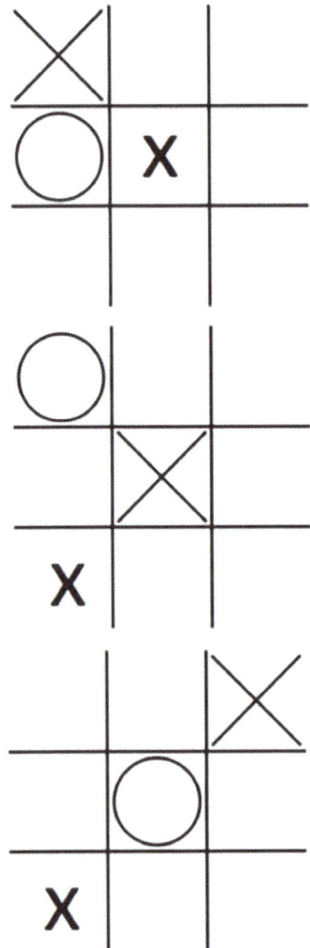

Lesson Plans

Short Description:

Goals and Objectives:

Students will learn that...

-
-
-

Students will be able to...

-
-
-

Materials needed:

-
-

Procedure:

Introduction (   ):

Activity (   ):

Activity - Discussion (   ):

Online Activity (   ):

Closure (   ):
Ask the students the following questions:

-
-
-

Lesson Plans

Functions

Short Description:

In this class students will be introduced to the concept of loops. They will interact with lengthy code and improve it by rewriting it using loops.

Goals and Objectives:

Students will learn that...
- Computers need very specific instructions
- There are many different ways to program
- How to use blockly
- Functions hold information

Students will be able to...
- Create a main function with correct syntax
- Navigate through Vox-L classroom effectively

Materials needed:
- Workbook Activity: Shape Collector
- Computers
- PDF Printed

Procedure:

Introduction
The lesson should begin with the instructor introducing him/herself to the class. The instructor should clarify that students are present to learn how to program and start a discussion on what it means to be a programmer. They should also explain the format of the class, describing the use of the workbook, as well as the hardware they will be using and Vox-L. Reassure students that the code that they will write works for Minecraft modding.

Activity
Have them complete Shape Collector activity. This activity is intended to have students start interacting with code following instructions and function calls. Each function is a set of instructions as they will see in the activity and the order in which the functions are called is very important.

Activity - Discussion
Ask students how they think the activity has to do with programming. After getting their responses try to tie in all the answers together and come up with a specific definition about functions that the whole class can understand.

Online Activity
Have the students complete the online activity by scanning the QR code.

Closure
Ask the students the following questions:
- What is a function?
- General question about Vox-L (controls, buttons, menus)

Lesson Plans

Functions Calls

Short Description:

This class will be used to reinforce the concept of functions and functions calls. They will also be introduced to the concept of ambiguity in programming. They will interact with various forms of instructions and see where they could go wrong.

Goals and Objectives:	Materials needed:
Students will learn that... • You can use more than one function • Functions should be named appropriately Students will be able to... • Create multiple working functions • Understand function call order effectively	• Workbook activity: Hanging with Jillian • Computers • PDF printed

Procedure:

Introduction
This lesson should begin with a quick review of what functions are. Ask students the following questions to make sure they understand functions:
- Can anyone tell me what function we always need in our program?
- What if we spell "main" with a capital "m", will it work? Why not?

Present the following scenario to the class.

You find a robot from another planet that has no idea what it's like to live on earth. This robot communicates by receiving instructions and saying "yes" or "no". It will simply stop working when it's confused. This robot has no idea what human things are so we have to be sure to explain in detail how they work. Let's teach this robot how to make a PB&J sandwich.

Continue this activity by following instructions in the attached handouts. As you work through this activity ask: "Will this build a sandwich".

Activity
Have them complete Hanging with Jillian activity. As they complete it, ask them to keep in mind where the instructions can go wrong. This concept is known as ambiguity in programming

Activity - Discussion
Go through each problem and ask students where the activity could go wrong.

Online Activity
Pass out the printed PDF so students can scan the QR code and complete the activity. Explain again that they do not need to add or remove any of the code for complete the activity successfully.

Closure
- Ask the students the following questions:
- What is the name of the function we always need?
- What is a function call?

Lesson Plans

Loops

Short Description:

In this class students will be introduced to the concept of loops. They will interact with lengthy code and improve it by rewriting it using loops.

Goals and Objectives:

Students will learn that...
- Code can be made shorter and easier to read with loops
- They are really helpful when building structures

Students will be able to...
- Repeat their code using the loop block
- How to refactor code

Materials needed:
- Workbook Activity: Lunch Time
- Computers
- PDF Printed

Procedure:

Introduction
This lesson should begin with a class-wide demonstration of a drone creating a tower of 10 blocks.
By this point students should understand how a series of drones can be given to a drone to place blocks. Present the long way to create a tower to students, and then ask them to observe what parts of the code are repeating. Explain that we can get rid of all those repeating blocks and instead use a loop to wrap the blocks that we want to repeat.

Activity
Have them complete Lunch Time activity.

Activity - Discussion
As they complete this activity, keep in mind the following questions to ask your students:
- Why are loops helpful?
- How would you use loops in your everyday life?

Online Activity
Pass out the PDF activity for students to work on. Have them load the code and complete the online activity.

Closure
Ask the students the following questions:
- Why are loops useful?
- What other mods can you think of where a loop would be necessary (beside building things)?

Lesson Plans

Nested Loops

Short Description:

In this class students will continue to work with loops. They will interact with code that already uses loops, and the idea is to loop the loop. This is useful when trying to build more complex functions.

Goals and Objectives:	**Materials needed:**
Students will learn that… <ul><li>Loops can also be repeated within themselves</li><li>How to build more complex structures</li></ul> Students will be able to… <ul><li>Repeat their code using the loop block</li></ul>	<ul><li>Workbook activity: Build the Structure 2.0</li><li>Computers</li><li>PDF printed</li></ul>

Procedure:

Introduction
This lesson should begin with a class-wide demonstration of a drone creating a tower of 10 blocks. By this point students should understand how to code this using loops. The goal is to build a 10x10 wall. Students will probably want to add 9 other loops that build a tower of 10 blocks (basically: loop of 10, make drone come down and move right, loop of 10, reset the drone, loop of 10, etc…). Explain to the class that we're basically repeating the loop of 10 and the moving the drone over and over. We can instead add an outer loop around these instructions and this will build a 10x10 wall.

Workbook Activity
Have them complete Build the Structure 2.0 activity.

Activity - Discussion
As they complete this activity, keep in mind the following questions to ask your students:
- How many square will this code fill-in?
- How can you differentiate the outer loop from the inner loop?

Online Activity
Pass out the PDF activity for students to work on. Have them load the code and complete the online activity.

Closure
Ask the students the following questions:
- How can I change the wall code to build a floor instead?
- Do you think I can use a triple nested loop? (to make a 10x10x10 cube)

Lesson Plans

Variables

Short Description:

In this class session students will learn that variables can hold more information that just drones. They can also be used to store strings, numbers, and booleans.

Goals and Objectives:	Materials needed:
Students will learn that... • Variables can hold information of various types. Students will be able to... • Use a variables for materials in drone block placing programs	• Workbook Activity: Find the Correct Lockers! • Computers • PDF Printed

Procedure:

Introduction
This lesson should begin with a class-wide demonstration of a drone creating a tower of 10 blocks of a specific material.
By this point students should understand how to use drones efficiently.
Rewrite the code in front of the class so the value of the material being placed is stored in a variable in the main function and the drone places the material variable. Explain that if the code were to create a complex structure and we wanted to change the material, instead of looking through the entire code changing every instance of the material, we can simply change the value of the variable.

Activity
Have them complete Find the Correct Lockers activity.

Online Activity
Pass out the PDF activity for students to work on. Have them load the code and complete the online activity.

Closure
Ask the students the following questions:
- How can variables make our code easy to modify?
- How do variables apply to your everyday life?

Lesson Plans

Parameters

Short Description:

In this class session students will learn about parameters. This is a more advanced use of variables that can be used to attach/expect information to a certain function.

Goals and Objectives:	Materials needed:
Students will learn that... • Parameters are variables that hold information for a specific function Students will be able to... • Create a function with parameters	• Workbook Activity: Help The Miners • Computers • PDF Printed

Procedure:

Introduction

This lesson should begin with a class-wide demonstration of building a tower. Revisit the day two demonstration of using variables to store the height of the tower. Now, parameters take storing information a bit further. Parameters are like variables that hold information for a specific function. Present the following analogy to explain variables Imagine a buildBurger function. Whenever you call the buildBurger function a burger will be cooked, but some burgers have different toppings. We can create parameters to declare that information in the function call. Possible parameters could be the following:
- Cheese: (true or false)
- Amount of patties: (number)
- Veggie: (true or false)
- Bread Type: (string)

Now whenever buildBurger function is called, the parameter information will have to be specified.

Activity

Have students complete Help the Miners activity.

Activity - Discussion

As they complete this activity, keep in mind the following questions to ask your students:
- What is the difference between a parameter and a variable?
- How would you use loops in your everyday life?

Online Activity

Pass out the PDF activity for students to work on. Have them scan the code and complete the online activity.

Lesson Plans

Logic

Short Description:

In this class students will learn about logic. This is a very important concept in coding. This section can be summarized in four simple words "if this, do that." This is what programmers use to set rules and conditions in their code.

Goals and Objectives:	**Materials needed:**
Students will learn that… <ul><li>Logic in code is used to set rules for our code.</li></ul> Students will be able to… <ul><li>Use a logic "if do" in their code efficiently.</li></ul>	<ul><li>Workbook Activity: Spare Change</li><li>Computers</li><li>PDF Printed</li></ul>

Procedure:

Introduction
This lesson should begin with a class-wide demonstration logic with coin flips. Explain how we can set rules for the outcomes of heads or tails, and that is the same way logic is used in code. "If the coin lands on tails, I get one point or else, I lose one point"

Activity
Have students complete the Safety First activity.

Activity - Discussion
As they complete this activity, keep in mind the following questions to ask your students:
- What is the difference between a parameter and a variable?
- How would you use loops in your everyday life?

Online Activity
Pass out the PDF activity for students to work on. Have them scan the code and complete the online activity.

Closure
Close the class with a discussion about what code they worked on by asking students the following questions:

What are some examples of logic in video games?
- Point systems
- Breaking a block in Minecraft
- Moving on to next levels in code

How does logic work in everyday life?
- If I press this button, this happens
- If I drop this pencil, then it will fall
- Encourage students to provide some examples of logic in real life

www.ingramcontent.com/pod-product-compliance
Lightning Source LLC
Chambersburg PA
CBHW042027150426
43198CB00002B/85